HowExpert

How To ~~~~ Feature Article

Your Step By Step Guide To Writing Feature Articles

HowExpert

Copyright HowExpert™
www.HowExpert.com

For more tips related to this topic, visit HowExpert.com/featurearticle.

Recommended Resources

- HowExpert.com – Quick 'How To' Guides on All Topics from A to Z by Everyday Experts.
- HowExpert.com/free – Free HowExpert Email Newsletter.
- HowExpert.com/books – HowExpert Books
- HowExpert.com/courses – HowExpert Courses
- HowExpert.com/clothing – HowExpert Clothing
- HowExpert.com/membership – HowExpert Membership Site
- HowExpert.com/affiliates – HowExpert Affiliate Program
- HowExpert.com/writers – Write About Your #1 Passion/Knowledge/Expertise & Become a HowExpert Author.
- HowExpert.com/resources – Additional HowExpert Recommended Resources
- YouTube.com/HowExpert – Subscribe to HowExpert YouTube.
- Instagram.com/HowExpert – Follow HowExpert on Instagram.
- Facebook.com/HowExpert – Follow HowExpert on Facebook.

Publisher's Foreword

Dear HowExpert reader,

HowExpert publishes quick 'how to' guides on all topics from A to Z by everyday experts.

At HowExpert, our mission is to discover, empower, and maximize talents of everyday people to ultimately make a positive impact in the world for all topics from A to Z...one everyday expert at a time!

All of our HowExpert guides are written by everyday people just like you and me who have a passion, knowledge, and expertise for a specific topic.

We take great pride in selecting everyday experts who have a passion, great writing skills, and knowledge about a topic that they love to be able to teach you about the topic you are also passionate about and eager to learn about.

We hope you get a lot of value from our HowExpert guides and it can make a positive impact in your life in some kind of way. All of our readers including you altogether help us continue living our mission of making a positive impact in the world for all spheres of influences from A to Z.

If you enjoyed one of our HowExpert guides, then please take a moment to send us your feedback from wherever you got this book.

Thank you and we wish you all the best in all aspects of life.

Sincerely,

BJ Min
Founder & Publisher of HowExpert
HowExpert.com

PS...If you are also interested in becoming a HowExpert author, then please visit our website at HowExpert.com/writers. Thank you & again, all the best!

COPYRIGHT, LEGAL NOTICE AND DISCLAIMER:

COPYRIGHT © BY HOWEXPERT™ (OWNED BY HOT METHODS). ALL RIGHTS RESERVED WORLDWIDE. NO PART OF THIS PUBLICATION MAY BE REPRODUCED IN ANY FORM OR BY ANY MEANS, INCLUDING SCANNING, PHOTOCOPYING, OR OTHERWISE WITHOUT PRIOR WRITTEN PERMISSION OF THE COPYRIGHT HOLDER.

DISCLAIMER AND TERMS OF USE: PLEASE NOTE THAT MUCH OF THIS PUBLICATION IS BASED ON PERSONAL EXPERIENCE AND ANECDOTAL EVIDENCE. ALTHOUGH THE AUTHOR AND PUBLISHER HAVE MADE EVERY REASONABLE ATTEMPT TO ACHIEVE COMPLETE ACCURACY OF THE CONTENT IN THIS GUIDE, THEY ASSUME NO RESPONSIBILITY FOR ERRORS OR OMISSIONS. ALSO, YOU SHOULD USE THIS INFORMATION AS YOU SEE FIT, AND AT YOUR OWN RISK. YOUR PARTICULAR SITUATION MAY NOT BE EXACTLY SUITED TO THE EXAMPLES ILLUSTRATED HERE; IN FACT, IT'S LIKELY THAT THEY WON'T BE THE SAME, AND YOU SHOULD ADJUST YOUR USE OF THE INFORMATION AND RECOMMENDATIONS ACCORDINGLY.

THE AUTHOR AND PUBLISHER DO NOT WARRANT THE PERFORMANCE, EFFECTIVENESS OR APPLICABILITY OF ANY SITES LISTED OR LINKED TO IN THIS BOOK. ALL LINKS ARE FOR INFORMATION PURPOSES ONLY AND ARE NOT WARRANTED FOR CONTENT, ACCURACY OR ANY OTHER IMPLIED OR EXPLICIT PURPOSE.

ANY TRADEMARKS, SERVICE MARKS, PRODUCT NAMES OR NAMED FEATURES ARE ASSUMED TO BE THE PROPERTY OF THEIR RESPECTIVE OWNERS, AND ARE USED ONLY FOR REFERENCE. THERE IS NO IMPLIED ENDORSEMENT IF WE USE ONE OF THESE TERMS.

NO PART OF THIS BOOK MAY BE REPRODUCED, STORED IN A RETRIEVAL SYSTEM, OR TRANSMITTED BY ANY OTHER MEANS: ELECTRONIC, MECHANICAL, PHOTOCOPYING, RECORDING, OR OTHERWISE, WITHOUT THE PRIOR WRITTEN PERMISSION OF THE AUTHOR.

ANY VIOLATION BY STEALING THIS BOOK OR DOWNLOADING OR SHARING IT ILLEGALLY WILL BE PROSECUTED BY LAWYERS TO THE FULLEST EXTENT. THIS PUBLICATION IS PROTECTED UNDER THE US COPYRIGHT ACT OF 1976 AND ALL OTHER APPLICABLE INTERNATIONAL, FEDERAL, STATE AND LOCAL LAWS AND ALL RIGHTS ARE RESERVED, INCLUDING RESALE RIGHTS: YOU ARE NOT ALLOWED TO GIVE OR SELL THIS GUIDE TO ANYONE ELSE.

THIS PUBLICATION IS DESIGNED TO PROVIDE ACCURATE AND AUTHORITATIVE INFORMATION WITH REGARD TO THE SUBJECT MATTER COVERED. IT IS SOLD WITH THE UNDERSTANDING THAT THE AUTHORS AND PUBLISHERS ARE NOT ENGAGED IN RENDERING LEGAL, FINANCIAL, OR OTHER PROFESSIONAL ADVICE. LAWS AND PRACTICES OFTEN VARY FROM STATE TO STATE AND IF LEGAL OR OTHER EXPERT ASSISTANCE IS REQUIRED, THE SERVICES OF A PROFESSIONAL SHOULD BE SOUGHT. THE AUTHORS AND PUBLISHER SPECIFICALLY DISCLAIM ANY LIABILITY THAT IS INCURRED FROM THE USE OR APPLICATION OF THE CONTENTS OF THIS BOOK.

COPYRIGHT BY HOWEXPERT™ (OWNED BY HOT METHODS)
ALL RIGHTS RESERVED WORLDWIDE.

Table of Contents

Recommended Resources 2
Publisher's Foreword 3
Introduction 8
  The Writer In You 9
  The Writing Process 10
    The Prewriting Stage 12
    The Writing Stage 13
    The Revising Stage 14
    The Proofreading Stage 15
    The Publishing Stage 15
  The Purpose Of Feature Articles 16
  What This Guide Is All About 17
Chapter 1: Sources Of Ideas For Feature Articles 18
    News Or Current Events 18
    Magazine Articles 18
    Observation 18
    Experience 19
    School Or University Campus 19
    Advertisements 19
    Special Events Or Occasions 19
    Movies 20
    Museums And Galleries 20
    Books 20
    TV And Radio 20
    Speeches 20
    Travels 21
    Conversations And Interviews 21
    Journals 21
    The World Around You—Your Environment 22
    Personal Infirmities 22
    Your Imagination 23
Chapter 2: Types Of Feature Articles 24
    Analysis Or Opinion On Current Events 24

Profiles Of Or Interviews With Well-Known People 24
Humorous Or Satirical Reflections 25
Personal Experience Or Anecdotes 25
Background Information On Local, National Or International Events 25
Human Interest Stories 25
Exposé 26
An Inspirational Article 26
A Historical Feature 26
Round-up 27

Chapter 3: How To Write Feature Articles ... 28
The Beginning Of A Feature *28*
Different Kinds Of Leads 28
Other Ways To Begin Your Feature *38*
The Body Of A Feature *43*
Chronological Pattern 43
Space Pattern 44
Logical Method 44
Cause(s) And Effect 44
Comparison And Contrast 45
Analogy 45
The Ending Of A Feature *46*
Summary Of The Article 47
Announcement Of The Main Point For The First Time 47
Question Left In Your Readers' Mind 47
Suggest Result(s) Or Significance 48
Forecast Or Prophecy 48
Repetition Of The Introduction 48
Repetition of a sentence or slogan, or a reference to the title 49
Quotation 49

Chapter 4: Tips When Writing Your Feature Articles 51
Focus On Human Interest 51

Be clear About Why You Are Writing The Article 51
Write In The Active Voice 51
Accuracy Is Important 52
Keep Your Audience Clearly In Mind. 52
Avoid clichés And Sentimental Statements 52
Avoid Lengthy, Complex Paragraphs. 53
Decide On The Tense Of Your Feature Story At The Start And Stick To It 53
Ideas Come From Everywhere 53

Chapter 5: Qualities Of A Good Feature Writer 54
Interest In People And Things Around You 54
Curiosity, Imagination, Sense Of Adventure 54
Technique Of A Fictionist 54
Ability To Write 55
Investigate 55
Know The Source 55
Best Titles 55
Tone 56
Know What Makes Up A Good Feature Article . 56
Know Your Readers 56

Chapter 6: How To Get Your Feature Articles Published 57
Read The Publication 57
Give A Proposal 57
Include Good Examples 57
Study The Editorial And Staff Writers' Pieces 57
Select Your Market 57
Send Good Quality Pictures 57
Submit Your Story Typed And Double-spaced ... 57
Follow Up The Status 58

Conclusion 59
Recommended Resources 61

Introduction

A feature article, sometimes known as a feature story or feature, is a special and important article in a magazine or newspaper. Such an article explores and presents varied issues, opinions, ideas, and experiences on a variety of interesting subjects.

Because a feature can take so many forms and can cover so many subjects, it is considered as a great kind of article because it attracts many different kinds of readers. Moreover, a feature has both similarities and differences to essays, news stories, or editorials.

First, a feature is different from an essay because it is based on facts rather than opinion. This is dissimilar to an ordinary essay you read or study in school.

Second, a feature is like a news story written to inform, but it magnifies the news in a leisurely and entertaining way. Unlike a news story which can quickly go out of date, a feature has a more general focus and retains interest after a few days or months. A feature article, therefore, may or may not be timely. Good ones are timeless. Moreover, writing features adds life to magazines, newspapers or websites, because you are allowed to use more creativity and show off more of your own style in writing features.

Finally, a feature is like an editorial because it is hung on a news peg. An editorial is heavy reading, however, while a feature is light reading. An editorial is meant to be an impersonal argument for or against a position while a feature allows expression of personal thoughts freely and spontaneously.

The Writer In You

Writing begins with you. It is a way for you to connect with the world outside you. When you write, you write to someone—for your readers—and you write to be read. Writing is a way for you to connect with your inner world—your world of thoughts, feelings, and dreams. Sometimes you write for others, and sometimes you write for yourself.

Writing is creating, and you are the creator. Writing is thinking, and it is discovering what you think on the page.

Thus, we write because writing is an extension of our language across and beyond time and borders. We write to express and explain our ideas when sometimes we find it hard to express them orally. But there is more to it than this when writing feature articles. Here what we do is like building a house. Like a brick, every word we choose to use should be the right and the most fitting one. Every word-brick we pick is placed in its proper place, and by then we will see the wall beginning to rise—every part of our house is taking its shape as we desire it to be.

For example, if this is our sentence: "<u>Placed on a large dish</u>, my daddy stood up to <u>cut</u> the ripe papaya"—the word, <u>cut</u>, is not the best fitting word to use. Although it is technically correct, <u>slice</u> gives more flavor to the writing instead. Also, the phrase <u>placed on a large dish</u> is misplaced in the sentence because, obviously, it makes it appear that the daddy was placed on the large dish rather than the papaya. So, in order not to make a funny sentence, <u>placed on a large dish</u> should be placed last and should not be placed first in our sentence. Hence, we now have a correct and sensible sentence: "My daddy stood up to slice the ripe papaya placed on a large dish."

We write hoping not to confuse our readers. We write because it is a way of finding out about our world, and it is a way to change it! That is a powerful thought. Writing, therefore, is powerful-- a powerful tool in our world!

The Writing Process

The writing process breaks writing into steps or stages. These stages are: prewriting, writing, revising, proofreading, and publishing. You may start with prewriting and end by publishing. However, you may go back and forth among the other stages or do two or more stages at once. As you become more familiar with the stages, you will feel more comfortable moving back and forth.

In the prewriting stage, you choose an object or subject to write about. You write all the things that would come into your mind related to and associated with your subject. They don't have to be organized, just get all the ideas down on paper.

In the writing stage, you are now ready to write the actual text. Sometimes, however, you do not know how to get started, and often, once you start, you do not know how to keep going. Nevertheless, just start writing. That is the important thing for you to do. Do not worry if your ideas are out of order or if you make spelling errors. You will be able to improve your writing when you revise and proofread it. You can begin your feature in so many ways. One is to begin with a question.

For example, "Is it a sin to be single or to choose to remain single for the rest of your life?" After you start, use your notes to explore all the possible answers to this question. Do not try to include everything you have jotted down, though. Pick and choose the most important points. Finally, add a conclusion to your write-up, such as, "So get the most of your single years. Bask in the bliss and freedom that the unwedded state offers. Enjoy it while it lasts."

Next is the revising stage. Revising allows you to spot a grammatical error, an ill-fitting adjective, or a libelous word. Reading out loud to yourself is an important revising strategy. First think about your purpose. Then think about your audience. Another revising strategy is sharing your article with a friend or with a family member. Read your writing aloud, and ask your listener to make suggestions and ask questions. Think about your friend's suggestions and make the changes which you feel help make the piece stronger.

After revising comes the proofreading stage. After you have made sure your article says what you want to say, proofread it for correctness. Check punctuation, indentations, word use, and spelling. While the computer can spell check your article for you, just because it was done automatically does not mean that the article is error-free. For example, when the word that you want to type is "called" but you have accidentally typed it as "culled", the computer will not mark it red because culled is also a proper English word. In addition, some of the grammatical changes the spell check suggests are wrong. Therefore, the best thing to do after spell-checking your article is to proofread it several times manually.

Finally, the last stage is publishing. You can now send it to a magazine, newspaper or website for possible publication.

To make the writing process clearer and more concrete, let us look at some examples:

The Prewriting Stage

One way to stimulate details for the subject of the feature article that you are planning to write is to have a conversation with a friend. Say you decide to write a story about an experience with an animal. Be sure that you narrate to him the complete story from start to finish and write down the details you brought to mind after the conversation.

This is how your prewriting notes may look:

Prewriting Notes

- Rode my bike home
- Saw a deer near bushes
- Deer: big, beautiful, smooth hide, tan

- Stared at me
- Me: excited, held my breath

If you have no friend or somebody to turn to who can listen to your story at the time when you are prewriting, you can also try jotting down the details of your encounter with a deer using an observation chart. In the chart you may write a tentative title for your article.

Now, this will be what your observation chart looks like:

Tentative Title: Meeting a Deer

What I saw: a doe, sleek hide, huge eyes, still as a statue

What I heard: a faint rustling, then silence

What I felt: surprised, excited, as if in a dream

The Writing Stage

Place your prewriting notes and observation chart in front of you. Then begin to write your feature article.

Here are ways to begin:

- Did I ever tell you about the time I found a _____?
- I could not believe my eyes when I saw the _____!

- "Be careful of stray animals," Mom told me, but _____.

Now, you can begin writing, and keep writing till you "finish" your story. Do not worry about mistakes. You can correct them later. In addition, you may change the first line of your feature later to something that has more impact. It's best to dive right in and get started and worry about revising later.

So, this is now your first draft. (Note that the errors in this draft are intentional because we are going to show you how to revise such errors in the next section.)

I could not believe my eyes! I had taken a new shortcut, and suddenly I found a deer munching <u>leafs.</u>

It had a smooth, tan hide and was taller than my bike. It was eating from the tall bushes next to the parking lot. I rode my bike closer. The deer looked up.

I said, "<u>hello</u>, you beautiful creature." I expected the deer to look, but it did not. It just stared at me with its <u>Large</u> brown eyes. Quietly, I got off my bike and placed it on the ground. When I looked up, the deer was gone.

The Revising Stage

Revising is making changes to improve your writing. How can you know if you need to make some changes? Here is a strategy that may help you decide:

- Read to yourself. Review your purpose. Did you write an article to amuse or entertain your audience?
- Think about your readers. Will they see what you saw? Hear what you heard? Feel what you felt?
- Decide which part of your feature story you like best, then expound upon it, highlight it, dramatize it.
- Have you used first-person point of view to make your readers see your story through your eyes?

The Proofreading Stage

This stage looks for and fixes errors. You can delete what is unnecessary and add what is lacking or important.

The Publishing Stage

This is now the final stage where you have made a printout of your article, which you have checked several times to make sure that it is error-free.

At this stage you now have a finished or final manuscript. See what you have corrected, deleted or changed, and what you have added.

My First Encounter with a Deer

I could not believe my eyes! I had taken a new shortcut, and suddenly I encountered a deer munching leaves. It was eating from the tall bushes next to the parking lot.

Have you ever seen a deer? It had a smooth, tan hide and was taller than my bike. I rode my bike closer. The deer looked up.

I said, "Hello, you beautiful creature." I expected the deer to bolt, but it did not. It just stared at me with its large brown eyes. Quietly, I got off my bike and placed it on the ground. When I looked up, the deer was gone. I felt as if I had been dreaming.

The Purpose Of Feature Articles

All articles either aim to inform, to entertain, or to persuade. Feature articles do not only inform, entertain, and persuade, though; they also interpret, and add depth and color to a news story. They may also instruct, advise, and invoke sympathy. In fact, besides these requirements, online articles must also grab your reader's attention quickly and hold that attention as much as possible until the end of your article.

Writing a great feature article, therefore, is not always easy, since there are many elements necessary to make up one great article that reads fluidly.

Finally, the purpose of a feature article varies depending on the media it is meant for. It should appeal to the particular readers it is serving or targeting. Hence, if the magazine or website is for middle-aged women, the article should reflect these women's interests in lifestyle, career, money, health and relationships.

What This Guide Is All About

This guide focuses first on the sources of ideas for feature articles, then their types. After that, the structure of a feature article, which includes its introduction, body, and conclusion, will follow. Next are specific tips for how to write a feature. After that, the qualities of a good feature will be enumerated. Finally, the last part we will cover is what you need to do to get your feature article published.

Chapter 1: Sources Of Ideas For Feature Articles

Before you start looking for ideas for your feature article, you should always consider your target readers of a particular publication because they will help you decide on what subject to write about.

News Or Current Events

Daily news is the number one source of ideas. It is always a must to know what is happening locally, nationally, and globally.

Magazine Articles

Reading and writing are inseparable. You must read and analyze magazine articles to get the feel of what editors want.

Observation

As a truly observant writer, you look into your own experiences and surroundings with the clear eye of a newcomer. You must learn to love the world around you and cultivate the spirit of adventurism.

Experience

Your experiences need not be unusual. Everyday experiences may often provide you article ideas which many of your readers can identify and relate with.

School Or University Campus

The myriads of activities in school are undeniably a rich source of ideas for your feature article.

Advertisements

Information about firms or companies engaged in trailblazing, innovative, or creative business ventures is another source of ideas for your feature. Read the business and trade journals of industries which interest you to find sources of ideas this way.

Special Events Or Occasions

Say yes to all the invitations you are able to. You may not only meet some new acquaintances who teach you about areas you're unfamiliar with, but you will also see how to put together events like this and be able to write about them.

Movies

Watch movies too, either in cinemas or at home.

Museums And Galleries

Visit these places and you may well spot a subject to write about.

Books

Read books of all sorts. You can visit other places you've never been by reading. Charles Dickens was an avid reader of books got ideas from the works of William Shakespeare, *The Arabian Nights*, and the old novels piled up in the attic of his home.

TV And Radio

Always be informed and stay updated about what is going on, both in the news and pop culture.

Speeches

Public speakers often talk about topical subjects so they're a great source of ideas for feature articles.

Travels

Go around and see as many other places as you can. Your travel to other places can give you ideas for writing a feature. Pearl S. Buck, for example, who was born in Hillsboro, West Virginia, spent most of her first sixteen years in Chinkiang, a city in the Yangtze River in China, when her missionary parents took her there. Not surprisingly, *Big Wave*, her story with Japanese characters, was written after her trip to Japan. If you don't have the means to travel far, even visiting a nearby city that you've never spent time in before can spark your imagination.

Conversations And Interviews

Talk, listen, and exchange ideas with people. Meet people, talk to them, exchange ideas, and share insights. These people and these exchanges may become characters and subjects for your feature articles. In fact, you can also write an article about the subject of the conversations of other people you have heard, listened to, or unintentionally eavesdropped upon.

Journals

A journal or diary is a series of your own personal writing pieces called entries. Always keep a journal to record and comment on your personal experience, to practice writing, and to collect a source of ideas for feature writing and even for other kinds of writing. Many famous writers have kept journals, including Selma Lagerlof of Sweden, the first woman to win the Nobel Prize for literature, and Anais Nin, who actually published her diaries to great acclaim.

The World Around You—Your Environment

Where you live, what you observe, and what you experience are very rich sources of ideas. Charles Dickens, for example, spent the happiest years of his childhood in Chatham, a dockyard town near London. He was a keen observer of the city life around him. He saw the inhumane conditions existing in the local hospitals, prisons, and poor houses. These experiences and observations inspired him to write such classics as *Oliver Twist, David Copperfield,* and *Great Expectations.*

Personal Infirmities

Surprisingly, when you are confined in a hospital or even just in your own room at home, you have the time to think freely and let your mind wander, and this freedom of thought may give you ideas that you would otherwise miss because you were too busy. In fact, if you have the urge to write, you should at least jot down some notes about your thoughts so that you will not forget them.

Your Imagination

Do not forget—this is the richest source of ideas.

Chapter 2: Types Of Feature Articles

The following are the various types of feature articles:

Analysis Or Opinion On Current Events

An example of this could be, "What I think about the one-child policy in China." Analysis or opinion articles usually revolve around a controversial or timely subject.

Profiles Of Or Interviews With Well-Known People

A very good example of this could be, "The techniques and secrets of Manny 'Pacman' Paquiao in boxing." Sometimes, however, you can interview a common person who has experienced an extraordinary event. For example, a child who was saved from kidnapping, a bystander who has foiled a rape or a vendor who has reported a robbery can all make for interesting stories.

Humorous Or Satirical Reflections

You can exaggerate and generalize here to heighten humor. However, you have to be careful with humor, as different people find different items humorous.

Personal Experience Or Anecdotes

Here, you can write about your very own experience— one that is unforgettable or one in which you gained some insight. You can also write about an anecdote you would like to share with your readers because it gives some lessons in life. Anecdotes help maintain your readers' interest.

Background Information On Local, National Or International Events

One example of this is a sport like zip lining. You can write about the longest dual zip line in Asia which can be found at Dahilayan Adventure Park in Manolo Fortich, Bukidnon, Philippines, and then this may lead to other stories about zip lining elsewhere.

Human Interest Stories

This type of article interests the greatest majority of readers. Write about a topic or subject that will attract and sustain your readers' interest. An example of this could be, "Ophiuchus, the 13th zodiac sign." With the advent of this new additional sign, most readers are surely interested to know what their new zodiac sign is now.

Exposé

This type of feature shocks or surprises your readers. For example, a piece that explains that people who use artificial sweeteners are more likely to gain weight than lose weight might qualify.

An Inspirational Article

Focusing on an inspirational point, this type of feature describes how to feel good or how to do good deeds that help other people. An example of this would be, "How poetry reading and writing can help cancer patients cope with their own feelings towards the disease."

A Historical Feature

This type of article focuses on a single aspect of the subject, and the details are arranged chronologically. One good example of such a topic is "how did legal gambling in the United States evolve?"

Round-up

This type focuses on one theme, such as losing weight. Here you can cite research and quotations, give opinions, and include anecdotes to round out the topic. An example of such an article would be "Weight Loss Made Easy."

You can submit any of these types of feature articles to a newspaper magazine or website that includes features, and get paid if the quality of the article is good and it matches the theme of the publication.

Chapter 3: How To Write Feature Articles

Unlike a news story, which uses an inverted pyramid, a feature article's geometric structure is more rectangular, as its beginning (introduction), middle (body), and end (conclusion) are equally important. In this case, you should make every part of the feature have equal weight or prominence as much as possible.

The Beginning Of A Feature

The beginning is crucial because it is where the reader will decide whether to read on or not. Here you have to entice your readers. Hook them. Use descriptions, questions, quotations, emotion, and drama.

Usually, the first or beginning sentence of your feature article is called the lead. There are different kinds of leads that you can choose from to begin your article.

Different Kinds Of Leads

1. Conventional Or Summary Lead.

    This lead is usually a summary of events. It answers as many as of the 5Ws and 1H—Who, What, Where, When, Why and How.

Here are some examples:

- <u>Who Lead</u>

    Example (1): *Elias Teves has a different way of seeing things in the army.*

    Example (2): *Eddie de la Cerna, a town official, still remembers how farming in his upland village used to be unproductive.*

- <u>What Lead</u>

    Example (1): *A TV commercial for a soft drink paved the way for her entrance into the world of modeling.*

    Example (2): *Cervical cancer is one of the most common cancers in women, next only to breast cancer.*

- <u>Where Lead</u>

    Example (1): *Zamboanga Peninsula, the largest manufacturer of canned sardines in the country, intends to keep its unofficial title as the bottled Spanish-style sardine capital of the Philippines.*

    Example (2): *The Quezon Memorial Circle will be the site for a 24-hour band concert to be held next week under the sponsorship of the San Miguel Corporation and the Quezon City government.*

- <u>When Lead</u>

Example (1): *Not too long ago, Mahathir Mohamad, then prime minister of Malaysia, did something unexpected.*

Example (2): *At the crack of dawn, John and his men finish sorting 100 kilos of live tiger grouper into watertight boxes and loading them into a motorboat docked alongside his house.*

- <u>Why Lead</u>

Example (1): *Why are deaths among post-coronary artery bypass graft surgery (CABG) patients with hypertension, diabetes, obesity, and high triglycerides higher in those without these co-morbid risks?*

Example (2): *Why not make good health priority number one in 2011?*

- <u>How Lead</u>

Example (1): *To cross the channel to the White Island, I took a motorized boat.*

Example (2): *Taking an early morning bath will perk you up and make you feel refreshed.*

1. **Unconventional Or Novelty Lead.**

This lead does not contain the gist of the story but merely serves as an opener into your feature. You can use this lead to make the data or information you have collected much more interesting by presenting it in a novel way so that you can arouse the curiosity and sustain the interest of your audience.

An unconventional lead can be any of the following:

- <u>Punch</u>

    This is short and terse. It emphasizes the situation and it is meant to startle or surprise your readers; thus, they are enticed to read the whole story of your article.

    Example (1): *Without gravity, everything floats. So how do astronauts do many of the same things they do every day at home?*

    Example (2): *Crime indeed does not pay. A 24-year old handyman was apprehended by the police after his rape victim told her father who was also a police officer.*

- <u>Quotation</u>

    You present here a direct quote from a person you have interviewed or talked to, and this becomes the main theme of your feature.

    Example (1): *My six-year old son Joseph once said that the reason why I am still alive is because I have a child like him praying all day and night. It was really touching.*

Example (2): *Maternal and child care means more than a safe pregnancy. It must go beyond that," says Mayor Perett.*

- Question

    You have to provoke and encourage your readers to go on reading your article to get the answer to the question you pose in the opening sentence.

    Example (1): *Who should benefit from the Marcos family wealth? Imelda Marcos believes that if her family can't retain all of its loot, the bulk should go to the government.*

    Example (2): *What is eco-spirituality? How does it differ from other forms of spirituality?*

- History Or Background

    Here you describe the event, or the person(s), or the place of a certain occasion.

    Example (1): *Every year in late April, people across the country celebrate Earth Day by volunteering their time or raising money to help protect and improve the environment.*

    Example (2): *What do Miley Cyrus, Miranda Cosgrove, and Zac Efron have in common? They all attended the 11th annual Teen Choice Awards, hosted by the Jonas Brothers, which took place on August 9, 2009.*

- <u>Cartridge Or Staccato</u>

    You use one, two, or three words in the opening that will make your readers go on reading to find out what the first three words are all about.

    Example (1): *Problems. Trials. Anxieties. We would rather live without them, yet they are always there.*

    Example (2): *Meetings. Exams. Grades computations. These did not prevent Dr. Eric Briones from attending a seminar-workshop on 'Managing Time in the 21st Century as a keynote speaker.*

- <u>Contrast</u>

    You point out opposites or extremes, or both, in opening your feature article.

    Example (1): *Sending messages back and forth over computers or cell phones can take a lot more time than having a quick conversation out loud.*

    Example (2): *Cancer is not a death sentence— it may even improve your life by giving you a reason to live each day to the fullest.*

- <u>Direct Address</u>

In your feature, you are actually addressing your readers, as if talking to them personally.

Example (1): *Forget about those onerous penalties for dipping into your certificate of deposit. More banks now let you withdraw from a CD before maturity, without paying a penalty.*

Example (2): *Does it often take you more than half an hour to fall asleep at night? Do you wake up frequently during the night, and sometimes too early in the morning, so that you have a hard time sleeping back again?*

- <u>Combination</u>

You combine two or more leads here, using the best elements of each. In fact, some leads of some feature articles are a combination. For instance, a **quotation lead** can be combined with a **history or background lead**, and a **question lead** can be combined with a **what** lead.

Example (1): *Over the years I often thought and wondered why a great variety of plants, vines and weeds have heart-shaped leaves," says Dr. Salvacion, a renowned physician working in a public hospital of the country, who was the guest speaker of the recently concluded conference on "Take Care of Your Heart on Valentine's Day.*

Example (2): *What do rocks in Pakistan, homes in the United States, and a park in Mexico have in common?*

2. **Grammatical-Beginning Lead**

   Although most leads start with the subject, you may start in some other way. Various grammatical structures not only give variety but also may help you present the proper relationships between facts, and add vigor to the structure of your lead.

Grammatical-beginning leads can be any of the following:

- Causal Cause

  This consists of a dependent clause beginning with 'because' or 'since'.

  Example (1): *Since he has already divorced his wife and is eager to move on, Peter has turned to the computer for a possible love match.*

  Example (2): *Because his townspeople's most pressing need is to earn a living, the mayor has instituted a new program to address their lack of capital.*

- Conditional Clause

  This also consists of a dependent clause beginning with 'if,' 'unless,' and 'provided'.

Example (1): *If operating costs are down, there will be no need to increase fares, and this will translate to lower transportation and delivery costs.*

Example (2): *Unless the weather improves, I won't go.*

- <u>Concessive Clause</u>

    You can begin your lead here with 'even though,' 'though' or 'although,' or 'despite.'

    Example (1): *Even though he is a close friend of the mayor, he didn't receive any special treatment.*

    Example (2): *Despite the fact that she served as president of the student government in her college years, she was still attracted to journalism rather than politics.*

- <u>Temporal Clause</u>

    This, too, consists of a dependent clause beginning with 'when,' 'while,' 'before,' 'since,' and 'as soon as.'

    Example (1): *When my friend didn't pay his rent for a second straight month, his landlord performed a defenestration on many of his belongings.*

Example (2): *While exploring the streets of Batan, I learned about a unique custom that was going to be enacted in a remote coastal town of Sabtang.*

- Infinitive Phrase

    This is a "to + verb phrase" lead.

    Example (1): *To solve the garbage problem and at the same time to raise income, city officials started a garbage recycling program.*

    Example (2): *To safeguard our health as best as we can is part of the stewardship of life.*

- Participial Phrase

    Here you have a choice to use a present participial phrase or a past participial phrase.

    Example: (1): *Wiping the steam off your bathroom mirror, you find yourself face to face with a huge pink dot on the tip of your nose.*

    Example (2): *Retired a month ago from being a professor in a university, Librada, who loved to feed stray cats at the lobby of her college, intends to go back to her hometown with her books inside her shoulder bag and a family of cats in a carton.*

- Prepositional Phrase

Your lead here is introduced by several prepositions such as like in, on, at, etc.

Example (1): *In rural communities, boys assist in the economic activities of their parents in a variety of ways.*

Example (2): *Among urban street children in Metro Manila and Cebu, common jobs include washing cars, shining shoes, and peddling cigarettes, newspapers and candies.*

- <u>Noun Clause</u>

This lead consists of a dependent clause which is used as the subject of the verb in the independent clause and begins with 'what,' 'how,' 'why,' 'whether,' and 'when.'

Example (1): *What she does for a living is not my concern.*

Example (2): *How we were ridiculed by the audience was both unbearable and unforgettable to us.*

Other Ways To Begin Your Feature

1. **Stating The Problem Or The Facts**

Example (1): *This is an answer to the rising cost of vegetables: raise your own.*

Example (2): *I admire lawyers. I like the way they dress up, walk, think, and argue. But most of all, I like their profession because it upholds the law.*

- <u>Begin With An Anecdote</u>—a short personal account of an incident or event.

    Example (1): *When I was seven years old, I broke my leg. I was swinging in the backyard, admiring the sky. Then suddenly the rope that held the swing came loose, and for a second I flew so high I thought I would never come down.*

    Example (2): *One day my cousin told me a man from a tribe nearby had taught him the technique of catching a python and taming it.*

- <u>Begin With An Aphorism, A Literary Or Biblical Allusion, And A Slogan.</u>

    Example (1): *"Water, water, everywhere, but not a drop to drink." This allusion from the Rime of the Ancient Mariner by Samuel Taylor Coleridge does not hold true anymore. Today, even flood water can quench your thirst.*

    Example (2): *"Breast is best." If this is true, then why are so many babies sucking bottles?*

- <u>Begin with an adverb or adverb phrase.</u>

    Example (1): *Tearfully, Terry retraced her steps home.*

    Example (2): *Into the dark woods the old man walks solitarily.*

- <u>Begin With An Appositive.</u>

    Example (1): *A country with hundreds of millions to feed, India has always been faced with food shortage.*

    Example (2): *A teen with strong determination to succeed, Tommy won in the Olympics.*

- <u>Begin By Transposition</u>, which means inverting the normal order of the sentence.

    Example (1): *To the victors belong the spoils.*

    Example (2): *Never have I spoken hurtful words to her.*

2. The Title

The very first thing that your readers will be attracted to is the title of your feature article. If your title is very catchy, chances are they will then start reading your article, especially when your lead is the kind that entices them to go on reading the whole article. If your title is flat or drab, or even worse, if it has a grammatical error, you have a slim chance or none at all to have some readership.

Good titles convey key information. Good titles help your readers identify the topic of your feature, and they can say whether it is something they should read or not.

When you are creating titles, remember that your readers are busy and overwhelmed by information sources so you have to put in extra effort to create something both informative and engaging.

How long should a good title be? Not too long but not too short.

Titles that will not work are those that lack a specific noun or subject. This also means that they lack a keyword or key phrase. So, when you write, focus on the single most important concept, idea, product, or topic in your article. Make sure that that concept or idea appears in the title too. If you can do this then you can ensure that you are on your way to making a better, more effective title.

Here are some titles for you to consider for your future feature articles:

- Grammatically Wrong

    Where Have All the Soldiers Go?

- Correct or Better

Where Have All the Soldiers Gone?

o <u>Quite Short</u>

Hearing Aids Prices

o <u>Not too Long, not too Short</u>

Hearing Aids Prices: Are Their Benefits Worth Their Costs?

Of course, there are some titles, though short, which are better and more effective too. For instance, the title A Doctor's Doctor matches its lead: Who treats doctors when they, too, are sick? There are also short titles that are good because they are alliterative, like: Model Mom and Forget Federalism.

Here are some other good titles from feature articles that I have read:

- *Blessing Behind Affliction*
- *In the Garden of Comfort and Healing*
- *A Heart for a Caregiver*
- *The Common Truth about the Common Cold*
- *A Spirit No Attack Can Ruin*
- *Holding on to an Empty Promise*
- *Sex is Not Like Tennis*
- *Suppose You Found a Watch…*

The Body Of A Feature

The body of your feature article is the substance of your message or your point. This contains the ideas that you want to convey to your audience.

The body of a feature article actually consists of a number of paragraphs that expound the main topic or theme of the article. **Usually this consists of:**

- Subheadings
- Facts and statistics which support your contention
- Personal viewpoints
- Opinions from authorities and experts
- Quotes and interviews
- Anecdotes and stories
- Specific names, places, and dates
- Photographs, tables, diagrams, graphs, and other graphic aids

You may not have all of these in one feature, but at least you have some of them to reinforce and prove your point.

You may organize the body of your article with the following techniques:

Chronological Pattern

This refers to the time order in which events naturally happen. If your feature follows this pattern, the event that takes place first is described first, and so on. You can use this pattern not only when your article tells a story but also when it describes a process.

Space Pattern

In this pattern, the main points of your article follow a spatial sequence. Here you illustrate the relationship of things in terms of space, say, from left to right, from top to bottom, from near to far, etc. in other words, in this method you describe the arrangement of things in a given place.

Logical Method

You can either develop the body of your article starting from a generalization to the specific or particular instances, or build up a generalization by proceeding from a particular to the general. In the first instance, you are using the deductive method, while in the second instance, you are using the inductive method.

Cause(s) And Effect

This technique tells why or how something happened and the result of the action. Here you examine the reasons for events or situations and their consequences. In presenting your ideas using this method to your readers, you must be careful that the factors, events, and incidents mentioned as having produced a definite result have really exerted a causal influence.

Comparison And Contrast

When you compare two things, you look at ways in which they are similar. When you contrast them, you look at ways in which they are different. You can develop the body of your article by pointing out the similarities and/or differences between two objects, persons, or even ideas that share some commonalities. In other words, here you are comparing and contrasting two **like** things—things that belong to the same genus or family. For instance, you can compare and contrast an orchid from a rose because they belong to the same genus—flowers. You make such concept vivid to your readers by making comparison with the simple and the familiar.

Analogy

This particular technique is different from comparison and contrast where you compare two **like** things. Here you compare two things, which while they are **unlike** because they belong to different genus, by pointing out their similarities in some respects. Analogy is particularly useful in clarifying something abstract and familiar by relating it to something concrete and familiar.

Actually, you can use more than one method in organizing the body of your article as long as you should observe the principles of unity, coherence, clarity, conciseness, and correctness.

You must remember that the body of a feature needs to keep any promises or answer any questions raised in the beginning or introduction. Here you discuss different opinions or you can explain your own. Do not forget to give examples and remember that if the tone of your feature article is serious, then, use real, empirical evidence rather than anecdotal evidence. In writing the body of your article, try to maintain an "atmosphere" throughout.

The Ending Of A Feature

The conclusion of your article is more apt to be remembered than what you have said in the body of your article. A good conclusion lingers in your readers' minds long after they have finished reading your feature. The last words impress your readers as strongly as the opening sentence. While the beginning draws your readers in, you should write the ending in such a way that they will remember the story of your feature.

You can conclude your article using any of the following ways:

Summary Of The Article

You tie up the loose ends, review the major ideas of your feature story, and point back to the lead.

Example: *Take it from the experts: smoking is definitely harmful to health. Smoking may make you feel manly, but you may not live long enough to be one.*

Announcement Of The Main Point For The First Time.

You can withhold out rightly stating the main point of your article until you reach the ending of it.

Example: *Therefore, a major part of the development communication effort should be directed at strengthening the character of the people and developing in them moral values, particularly self-discipline, self-reliance, strength of character, and fortitude.*

Question Left In Your Readers' Mind

Challenge your readers by posing a question (sometimes a rhetorical one) at the end of your article.

Example: *But is it not the role of society—through its government, through its public administration system—to address poverty, conflict, and the inequities of history?*

Suggest Result(s) Or Significance

You offer or give a concrete example of a result, or perhaps cite something that is of emotional importance to your readers.

Example: *Let us conserve our forests now if we want to save the future of our country, of our earth, of our children, and of our children's children.*

Forecast Or Prophecy

Be like a prophet and prophesy what would happen in the future, then tell this to your readers.

Example: *In six and a half centuries from now, if the population explosion is not checked, there will be one person standing on every square foot of land on earth. By that time, people will be devouring one another, for there will be no more space for plants to grow.*

Repetition Of The Introduction

You can repeat a statement in your introduction to end your article.

Example: _Bringing the house down_ is a funny way of conveying the message that we are sometimes given gifts by the most unlikely people that we tend to ignore. In the end, the unlikely pair has a chance to elevate each other's lives on higher ground if they don't end up _bringing the house down_.

Repetition of a sentence or slogan, or a reference to the title

Here you can also reiterate a particular statement or slogan, or some word that harks back to the title of your article.

Example: *Somebody aptly called us hospice care workers as 'midwives of the soul', because as midwives bring babies into the world, we help bring souls to heaven.* (The title of the feature is "Midwife of the Soul").

Quotation

Take a quotation from a text or from a pronouncement of a respected and credible person. The quotation should be appropriate and it should summarize the main point(s) of your article.

Example: To end this reflection, may I quote from the German poet, Rainer Maria Rilke: *'I find you, Lord, in all things and in all fellow creatures, pulsing with your life: as a tiny seed you sleep in what is small and in the vast you vastly yield yourself.'*

The wondrous game that power plays with things is to move in such submission through the world: groping in roots and growing thick in trunks and in treetops like a rising from the dead.'

Finally, you can combine two or more of these ways to end your feature. But remember to be creative in devising a vivid, forceful conclusion.

Chapter 4: Tips When Writing Your Feature Articles

Here are some of the things you must remember when beginning to write your feature article.

Focus On Human Interest

The feeling and emotions you put into your article are critical. Do not venture to write a science story unless you are writing for a science journal or magazine. Think about writing a human interest story.

Be clear About Why You Are Writing The Article

Is it to inform, persuade or convince, instruct, entertain, or to evoke emotion?

Write In The Active Voice

In active writing, people do things. Passive sentences often have the person doing the action at the end of the sentence or things being done by someone. Compare: "The boy kissed me" and "I was kissed by the boy"—the first sentence is active, the second one is passive.

Accuracy Is Important

You can interpret and elaborate but do not cheat or falsify. Accuracy means getting the correct information. So, when you interview someone, for example, ask his name, address and contact number. Never assume you know something. An interview needs to be in-depth and in person rather than over the phone because this will enable you to add color and detail. If your subject is unfamiliar to you, or someone on which you have no background, check with one or several experts before you write the first word. And when you use statistical data, you should double-check the figures.

Keep Your Audience Clearly In Mind.

What are their desires? What really matters to them?

Avoid clichés And Sentimental Statements

Especially at the end of your article.

Avoid Lengthy, Complex Paragraphs.

Decide On The Tense Of Your Feature Story At The Start And Stick To It

Present tense usually works. But of course, you should know when another tense is more appropriate. Shifting tenses is only appropriate within dialog, such as in an interview where your subject is explaining something that happened in the past.

Ideas Come From Everywhere

So watch, read, listen, keep up to date, and take down notes.

Chapter 5: Qualities Of A Good Feature Writer

As a good feature writer you have the following qualities that distinguish you from other writers.

Interest In People And Things Around You

Hence, you must be observant and must have a sharp eye to spot opportunities which can provide you with a subject matter that you can write about.

Curiosity, Imagination, Sense Of Adventure

And willingness to explore what is beyond the superficial.

Technique Of A Fictionist

Especially in relation to diction, unity of impression, dialogue, point of view, suspense, and climax.

Ability To Write

Since feature stories are less stereotyped in form and style than news stories, you are required to have more skill to write feature articles. In short, you must have some professional writing know-how (e.g., devices and patterns).

Investigate

Investigate every single angle before starting to write the story behind the story.

Know The Source

As a good feature writer you know the sources of ideas for your feature articles.

Best Titles

As a good feature writer, you know that the best titles for articles are both informative and intriguing.

Tone

As a good feature writer, you know what tone to use to a given topic or subject that you have chosen.

Know What Makes Up A Good Feature Article

You know how to keep your readers engaged by using language that sparkles, use humor to perk them up, and mention controversies that will emotionally engage them.

Know Your Readers

Finally, you know who your readers are because you are effective.

Chapter 6: How To Get Your Feature Articles Published

The last thing that you will do when you have already written and edited your article is to find a publishing outlet. Here are the things that you will do then to get your features published:

<u>Read The Publication</u> (magazine, newspaper, or maybe online) you want to write for.

<u>Give A Proposal</u> or a full article provided that this is superbly written.

<u>Include Good Examples</u> of your previously published articles. Write what editors what to publish, not what you want to write.

<u>Study The Editorial And Staff Writers' Pieces</u> They are aimed precisely at the publication's target audience.

<u>Select Your Market.</u> You can list a number of them that might buy your work, and study them for tips.

<u>Send Good Quality Pictures</u>, for pictures can help sell your story.

<u>Submit Your Story Typed And Double-spaced</u>.

Follow Up The Status of your sent article by a phone call after a week or two.

If a certain publishing agency does not want to use it, send it to others.

Now, you are all ready to write your articles! Good luck!

Conclusion

Generally, writing is not an easy hobby or way to make a living. If you write, you have to read, too, because reading and writing are inseparable. You might say that reading is your input while writing is your output. Then, when you write, there are many things that you should go through to become a writer.

If you want to become a published writer, then you have to learn the trade by heart. You must remember that writing has five stages. In these stages you should spare time to revise, edit, and proofread your work.

Specifically, to be a feature writer, there are many things that you have to consider aside from the writing stages. You have to pick your subject—one that will interest your readers. To begin your feature is also very tricky because you have to choose the best lead to use in your article. Titling your feature story also is a pain in the neck. The title should be one that would grab the readers' attention and entice them to read the whole article.

Almost everything is considered in writing a feature—the words that you are going to use, the tone of your language, the lead that you will use to begin your article, the organization of the whole feature, and the ending. The ending is not just a sort of a fairy tale ending as in, "And they lived happily ever after." And although you have already concluded your feature, that is not yet the end of the process. You still have to revise it, edit it, proofread it, and polish it. But all these efforts will be paid off the moment you will see your byline in a newspaper or magazine where you submit your article for publication. The happiness that you will feel upon seeing your name is priceless!

Recommended Resources

- HowExpert.com – Quick 'How To' Guides on All Topics from A to Z by Everyday Experts.
- HowExpert.com/free – Free HowExpert Email Newsletter.
- HowExpert.com/books – HowExpert Books
- HowExpert.com/courses – HowExpert Courses
- HowExpert.com/clothing – HowExpert Clothing
- HowExpert.com/membership – HowExpert Membership Site
- HowExpert.com/affiliates – HowExpert Affiliate Program
- HowExpert.com/writers – Write About Your #1 Passion/Knowledge/Expertise & Become a HowExpert Author.
- HowExpert.com/resources – Additional HowExpert Recommended Resources
- YouTube.com/HowExpert – Subscribe to HowExpert YouTube.
- Instagram.com/HowExpert – Follow HowExpert on Instagram.
- Facebook.com/HowExpert – Follow HowExpert on Facebook.

Printed in Great Britain
by Amazon